CLEVELAND'S
GOSPEL MUSIC

D1567551

UNIDENTIFIED FAMILY. This photograph of an unidentified family dressed in their Sunday attire is symbolic of the strong Black Christian family of the 1940s. Migrating from the south in search of greater economic opportunities and freedom, families such as this one came to Cleveland, bringing with them their strong religious values and traditions, including Gospel music. (Courtesy of Virginia Cross.)

On The Cover: THE MIGHTY REDEEMERS IN THE 1960s. See page 27 for a full description of this picture.

BLACK AMERICA SERIES

CLEVELAND'S GOSPEL MUSIC

Frederick Burton

ARCADIA
PUBLISHING

Copyright © 2003 by Frederick Burton.
ISBN 978-0-73853200-4

Published by Arcadia Publishing
Charleston, South Carolina

Printed in the United States of America

Library of Congress Catalog Card Number: 2003111068

For all general information contact Arcadia Publishing at:
Telephone 843-853-2070
Fax 843-853-0044
E-mail sales@arcadiapublishing.com
For customer service and orders:
Toll-Free 1-888-313-2665

Visit us on the Internet at www.arcadiapublishing.com

CONTENTS

ACKNOWLEDGMENTS

I thank God first and foremost for saving my soul a long time ago and keeping me to this day. I acknowledge my lovely wife, Benita, and my parents, Yvonne and Dub, for their continuous love and support in all of my efforts. My children, grandchildren, siblings, and their families are a constant source of love, inspiration, and enrichment. I love you more than words can say.

By way of this collection of photographs and images of Cleveland's Gospel music pioneers, I make a humble attempt to acknowledge some very special people of God who have labored, albeit in love, for nearly a century in singing and promoting Gospel music. I witnessed as an impressionable young boy the pride and dedication with which they sang God's praises. As a young man, I walked briefly in their shoes. This book is an expression of my deep gratitude for their examples and for the people in my life who have encouraged me along the way. I hope this small recognition is a blessing to them and their families and friends.

I'm fond of the story of Zerubbabel, the head of the tribe of Judah at the time of their return to Jerusalem after a 70-year Babylonian captivity. Zerubbabel's great task was to rebuild the temple, but the work was dogged by danger from the outside and discouragement from within. God gave him a vision to strengthen his faith. It had real meaning for him, and it contains a great principle for you and for me. "Not by might, nor by power, but by my spirit saith the Lord of hosts" (Zechariah 4:6). I encourage all who read this book to continue in this kind of faith, which is the only kind that can overcome the greatest of adversities and struggles.

INTRODUCTION

The church was on fire with the Holy Ghost, and the group sang "I Can't Even Walk Without Him Holding My Hand." Five blind men made up this group, and the song couldn't be more apropos. These men were the Five Blind Boys of Mississippi, and my dad and I were watching their performance through a window; admission into Saint Matthews Methodist Church on East Eighty-Sixth and Wade Park was $4, and we couldn't afford it. This was the first Gospel concert that I ever attended—the year was 1966, and Gospel music was hot! Nationally known groups like the Five Blind Boys and the Mighty Clouds of Joy were packing out churches across the country. During this time, talented Gospel groups emerged from backyards in and around Cleveland, Ohio. I would later learn that this emergence began its roots in Cleveland decades before I came along.

These groups didn't sing for money or fame. They performed every Sunday in front of as few as two souls, yet sang to the glory of God with all their heart as if their very lives depended on the performance, and there were thousands of souls in waiting. These groups sang beyond the point at which their exhaustion was clearly evident. Yet they sang all the more. Common was the white handkerchief that accompanied every lead singer, who despite his or her efforts to wipe away the ever present sweat, walked away from every performance with clothes soaked clear through to the bone. Paper fans on Popsicle sticks donning the image of Dr. King and area funeral homes were sometimes interesting to look at, but were no match for the heat that was generated from these energized song services. I often wondered what made them do what they did. I didn't realize until years later that they didn't have a choice in singing the Gospel; God had given them the gift, and they had to use it or lose it. Singing for some 60 and 70 years, these groups were great examples for many of the younger singers who struggled to find their way, myself included. Sunday after Sunday they suited up with excitement and anticipation to sing *just one more time*. Under a cloud of oppressive socio-economic conditions during the formative years, these Gospel singers touched the lives of thousands of people and inspired them with the hope of the good news of Jesus Christ. Among this collection of images is a glimpse of life in Cleveland during these challenging times in our history.

Cleveland is home to many talented solo vocalists, choirs, musicians, and songwriters, without whom Gospel music in Cleveland would not have taken root. Their contributions will have an everlasting impact here. The focus of this book, however, is on that body of singers who are called the "quartets"—not so called for the number of people in the group, but for their unique style of singing in smaller numbers than would be found with a choir or ensemble. This book also recognizes those radio announcers and promoters who, along with Gospel quartet singers, helped to establish Cleveland as a Gospel singer's metropolis. These individuals are a part of the history of Cleveland and a major part of Cleveland's Black community.

—Frederick Burton

One

GOSPEL MUSIC DURING THE EARLY AND DEPRESSION YEARS

CONSTRUCTION OF TERMINAL TOWER, DOWNTOWN CLEVELAND, C. 1920. Marking the progression of economic times in Cleveland, city planners began construction of the Terminal Tower, an office building standing 708 feet tall above the Cleveland Union Terminal in the 1920s, which the *Encyclopedia of Cleveland History* (1996) contends was "the tallest building in the world outside New York until 1967." The promise of prosperity and better living led to the migration of Black Americans to Cleveland in the 1920s and 1930s and spurred the popularity of Gospel quartet music here. While severe economic times during the latter part of the 1920s through the mid-1930s crippled growth for Americans in general, a growing community of Black Americans sang glorious and triumphant praises to God Almighty, surviving the tough economic times, racial separation, and the depression era. Their survival was due, at least in part for some and entirely for others, to the refuge that could be found in the "good news" delivered in songs that were sung a capella. (Courtesy of the Cleveland Public Library.)

9

THE CLEVELAND COLOURED QUINTET. God had something much greater in mind for this exceptional group of five Black men who formed as a quintet in 1913 with the intent to sing only in their local church. So dedicated to their calling were they that they made great personal sacrifices, giving up their secular employment and leaving loved ones to travel extensively throughout the United States, Canada, and Europe singing Gospel music and telling their testimony. Their extensive travel notwithstanding, the quintet was exceptional in that they sang with instrumental accompaniment during these early years. An account of their incredible journey was published in *The Coloured Quintet, A Narrative of God's Marvellous Dealings with the Cleveland Gospel Quintet and Their Personal Testimony* (John Ritchie, Ltd., 1937) This photograph was taken in December 1948. (Courtesy of The Western Reserve Historical Society.)

THE HUMBLE GOSPEL SINGERS. The Humble Singers are believed to be one of the first female Gospel groups in Cleveland, whose formation pre-dates 1928. (Courtesy of Marva Bright.)

THE SHIELDS BROTHERS. Beginning to sing together as a group in 1928, these distinguished gentlemen paved the way for Black Gospel quartet music in Cleveland with their sweet harmonious voices and did so consistently for some 70 years. (Courtesy of Gloria Webb.)

THE SHIELDS BROTHERS. This picture of the Shields Brothers is believed to have been taken in the 1960s. The Shields Brothers were frequent guest singers on Gospel radio and were known by their popular theme song "When the Roll is Called In Heaven I'll Be There." Pictured here from left to right are Lee Crosby, Arthur Beasley, James Henderson, Arthur Turner, and Claude Shields, Sr. (Courtesy of Claude Shields, Jr.)

THE JUBILEE FOUR, EARLY 1930s. Pictured here with a trophy won in a competition for enunciation, appearance, stage performance, and harmony, the Jubilee Four was a group of two sets of brothers and a neighbor who began singing together shortly before this picture was taken until 1944, when three members of the group were drafted to serve in World War II. Committed to singing the Gospel, the group resumed in 1946, following the war. From left to right are Clifford Phelps, William Phelps, Eugene Ross, Johnny Shields, and Claude Shields, Jr. Members William, Eugene, and Claude continue to sing today under the name of the Shields Brothers, inherited after all the members of the original Shields Brothers passed on. (Courtesy of Claude Shields, Jr.)

THE VOICES OF LOVE QUARTET. Pictured here in an animated fashion are the Voices of Love Quartet of Ebenezer Baptist Church in Cleveland. The group's theme song was "I'll Let Nothing Separate Me From His Love." Beginning with the front row from left to right are H.C. Hamilton, Fletcher Pippins (Manager), Alexander Lark, S.B. Bogan, and Willie Davis. (Courtesy of Virginia Cross.)

THE DEEP RIVER SONGBIRDS. Formed in 1935, the Deep River Songbirds went on to become one of the more familiar female Gospel groups in Cleveland. During their productive years in the 1940s and 1950s, the Deep River Songbirds were heard on the Gene Carroll Amateur Hour, where they earned Second Prize and several 13-week singing contracts on local radio stations including WHK, WJW, WJMO, and WGAR. Celebrating their 25th anniversary in 1960, the Deep River Songbirds retired as a group. Pictured here in 1938 are original members from left to right: Ruth Wallace, Cornell Thompson, Beatrice Addie, Josephine Wilkes, Primel Wilkes, and Eloise Burnett. (Courtesy of Eloise Burnett.)

GOSPEL CONCERT ADMISSION TICKET. This ticket was for admission to a 1957 Gospel program, one of many Gospel concerts featuring the Deep River Songbirds. (Courtesy of Eloise Burnett.)

THE DEEP RIVER SONGBIRDS. In 1938, while in competitive concert with out-of-town singers, the Deep River Songbirds earned First Prize. The Silver Cup is held here by James Huff, once known as the "granddaddy" of religious quartet, the group's founder, organizer, and instructor. Pictured on the front row from left to right are Beatrice Addie and Ruth Wallace. In the back row from left to right are Esther Woods, Josephine Wilkes, Eloise Burnett, and Cornell Thompson. (Courtesy of Eloise Burnett.)

THE DEEP RIVER SONGBIRDS. Playing a significant role in the introduction of color television in Cleveland, the Deep River Songbirds are pictured here at the Home and Flower Show at the Cleveland Public Auditorium during the week of December 17, 1947, where they sang spirituals for five consecutive nights. They were temporarily known as "The Blue Angels" for the color of their beautiful gowns. Pictured here from left to right are Beatrice Addie, Esther Woods, Eloise Burnett, Odessa Still, Josephine Wilkes, and Ruth Wallace. (Courtesy of Eloise Burnett.)

THE VOICES OF LOVE SEXTET. The Voices of Love Sextet, which consisted of all of the members of the Voices of Love Quartet, were affiliated with The Community Spiritualist Church of Christ, Inc. The group's favorite song was "Does Jesus Care," and their motto was "I will lift up mine eyes unto the mountains from whence shall my help come" (Psalm 121:1) and "Thy Word is a lamp unto my feet and light unto my path" (Psalm 119:105–106). Pictured from left to right are Alexander Lark, Fletcher Pippins (Manager), S.B. Bogan, Willie Davis, Leroy Aiken, and H.C. Hamilton. (Courtesy of Virginia Cross.)

THE BLUE RIBBON SIX. The Blue Ribbon Six began singing together in the 1930s. Pictured here in 1946, are from the front left to right, Jimmie Weems, Ollie Billings, Willie Belle Gervin, Eva Grier, Fannie Blure, Juanita Stewart, and Mildred Jones. (Courtesy Ollie Billings.)

THE ELITE JEWELS. This photograph of the Elite Jewels is believed to be one of the earliest professional photographs of this famed group of women who began singing together in 1936. Under the management of LeRoy Gaynor in 1937, the group began its traveling singing ministry. Etta Mae Hurd (far right) was daughter of co-founder Johnnie Feagan. Mildred Blair is on the far left, and Agnes Jackson is to her right. Pictured in front center is Senester Whatley. (Courtesy of Willie Mae Reese.)

THE ELITE JEWELS. Recipients of numerous trophies and plaques, the Elite Jewels were widely recognized throughout the United States for their traveling ministry, their many television appearances, and Gospel music recordings such as "I Was Standing by the Bedside of a Neighbor." The Elite Jewels were managed by famed Gospel promoter Arthur Turner for some 57 years before he retired. Pictured here adorning beautiful gowns are Maggie Cannone (seated in front) and from left to right in the back row are Mildred Blair, Agnes Jackson, Etta Mae Hurd, Senester Whatley, and Edith Jones. (Courtesy of Willie Mae Reese.)

THE ELITE JEWELS. Truly living up to their name, the Elite Jewels loaned their harmonious jewels at countless Gospel programs and music events over a half-century. These "Songbirds of the North," as they became known, are pictured here in 1964, in front from left to right: Etta Mae Hurd, Maggie Cannone, Edith Jones, Dolores Williams, and Mildred Blair. (Courtesy of Willie Mae Reese.)

"THE ELITE JEWELS"
61st ANNIVERSARY

OCTOBER 26, 1997

" SONG BIRDS OF THE NORTH"

PROGRAM SOUVENIR BOOKLET. This is a souvenir booklet from the Elite Jewel's 61st singing anniversary held in 1997. With the addition of new members over the years, the Elite Jewels continue to be a presence in Gospel music in Cleveland today, celebrating their 67th anniversary in 2003 under the leadership of Willie Mae Reese. (Courtesy of Willie Mae Reese.)

GOD SPEED THE DAY

We wondered for a long while, how long it would be before our nation would be brought into this world conflict. By now we know that the days of peace are for a time, at least, ended. And while we know that we are engaged in a righteous cause, yet we feel the unrest that war inevitably stirs in our hearts. How much we do need an inner purging now! How close must all of us feel God around us! Let us keep the fire of true religion burning in our breasts and let us, as we bow tonight, and as we bow in the future, say, "Thy will, O God, be done!" Let us pray.

O Thou eternal God, Thou alone knowest what is in store for us. The distant unknown is dismal and dark; but we feel that the God who watches over His own, slumbers not nor sleeps; and the Captain who has never lost a battle will see His children through. God speed the day when righteousness, and justice, and freedom, shall spread over all mankind, and when bigotry, hatred, prejudice, pride, injustice, greed, and sin, shall perish from the earth. Forgive us all our sins. Bless, we pray Thee, those who mourn for the loss of loved ones, and all who are confined upon their sick beds or in prison cells. Bless the President of these United States in this, his crucial hour, and GOD BLESS AMERICA. In Jesus' name we ask all this—Amen.

Words of Ralph Mark Gilbert (1899–1956) in 1941, who served as pastor of Pilgrim Baptist Church (South Bend, Indiana), Second Baptist Church (Dresden, Canada), and most prominently First African Baptist Church (Savannah, Georgia) from 1939 until his death. He was a prolific writer and producer of religious plays, a distinguished preacher, and a courageous fighter for civil rights in the 1930s and 1940s.

Two

GOSPEL MUSIC DURING THE WAR YEARS

THE DRAFT. In addition to the growing popularity of Gospel singing groups in the 1940s, Gospel music in Cleveland grew with great intensity under the cloud of World War II. This is a picture of men waiting in line at the draft board. Some young lead singers were drafted into the war, which had varying impacts on the groups left behind. Lines like these were common throughout the United States during World War II. More Black Americans sought refuge in the Gospel, oratorical and lyrical. The unique singing style and flamboyant image of Gospel quartet groups had wide appeal and laid the seed for commercial adventures for decades to come. (Courtesy of the Cleveland Public Library.)

THE ANGELS OF HARMONY. A popular Gospel group in the 1940s. Pictured here in the back row from left to right are Clinton Levert, Denver Wilborn, and Hiawatha Nowden. (Courtesy of Denver Wilborn.)

THE ELEY SISTERS. Photographed here from left to right are Rose Pressley, Willie Pressley, Joenida Eley, Hattie Eley, Grace Eley, and Jessie Eley. (Courtesy of Eloise Burnett.)

THE SUNSET FOUR.
Pictured here are
Madie Latimore (front row
left), Mary Marcus (front
center), and Lonnie Callahan
(back row right). (Courtesy
of Virginia Cross.)

THE L&N SINGERS. The L&N Singers organized as a group in the 1940s under the direction of Mr. Glover. The group was well known for their traditional jubilee sound of fast tempos and four-part harmony. (Courtesy of Robert Glover.)

THE GOLDEN ECHOES, c. 1960. Organized under the direction of Albert "Peg" Scott, this group made its Gospel music debut in 1940. At that time, the group was called the Five Golden Echoes, but expansion made it necessary to change their name. In 1966, the group recorded its first album for Checker Records. Pictured here from the front left to right are Pete Wilson, Albert "Peg" Scott, Jesse Allen, Jimmy Hughes, Frank Parks, Louis Patrick, Robert Lewis, and unidentified. (Courtesy of Virginia Cross.)

THE THOMAS BROTHERS. This
family group was organized in
1944, with four brothers, their
brother-in-law, and their nephew.
Pictured here on the far left is
Papa Joe (now a singer with the
Cleveland All Stars), and seated
on the far right is Alex Thomas.
(Courtesy of Alex Thomas.)

THE QUEENS OF HARMONY. This group was founded in 1940, in the home of Mrs. Ann Ridgeway (far right). Today's members include Nele Esbey (Tenor), Margaret ? (Lead Singer and Baritone), Loretta Hearling (Tenor, far left), and Linda Whiteside (fifth Singer). (Courtesy of Loretta Hearling.)

THE HARMONY ECHOES. Pictured here with the Harmony Echoes are Leroy Gaynor (standing left) and Clifford Phelps (seated on the left with hands crossed). Mr. Gaynor was a popular music director and radio announcer. Mr. Phelps was a member of the Jubilee Four in the 1930s. (Courtesy of the Call and Post Newspapers.)

THE TRAVELING STARS. Many Gospel ensembles and quartets were formed and began traveling to the east and west to meet the increasing demand for this new movement of religious music. (Courtesy of Elizabeth Kinney.)

THE MIGHTY REDEEMERS. This group sang together for some 40 years. This picture of them is believed to have been taken in the 1960s. Known for great song writing, the group was one of the few to sign with Peacock Records. Pictured from left to right are Joe Charlie, Albert Lee, Reverend Mitsy, T.J. McCallister (founder of the group), Sonny Martin, and Chuck Nelson. (Courtesy of Ann Dudley.)

THE SPIRITS OF HEAVEN GOSPEL SINGERS. Pictured here are the Spirits of Heaven with a familiar pose made famous by the R&B group The Temptations. (Courtesy of Virginia Cross.)

THE SOUL REVIVERS. This group began singing in the 1940s. Reverend Henry Brown (far left) began singing with the group some time in the 1950s. (Courtesy of Marva Bright.)

THE MIGHTY WINGS. This group was known for blessing the congregation with their theme song "Who Are We? The Mighty, Mighty Wings." Pictured here from left to right are Mitch ?, Jones ?, John ?, and Jake Webb. (Courtesy of Marva Bright.)

A Pastoral Prayer

O God, our Heavenly Father, we thank thee for this golden privilege to worship thee, the only true God of the universe. We come to thee today, grateful that thou hast kept us through the long night of the past and ushered us into the challenge of the present and the bright hope of the future. We are mindful, O God, that man cannot save himself, for man is not the measure of things and humanity is not God. Bound by our chains of sins and finiteness, we know we need a Savior. We thank thee, O God, for the spiritual nature of man. We are in nature but we live above nature. Help us never to let anybody or any condition pull us so low as to cause us to hate. Give us strength to love our enemies and to do good to those who despitefully use us and persecute us. We thank thee for thy Church, founded upon thy Word, that challenges us to do more than sing and pray, but go out and work as though the very answer to our prayers depended on us and not upon thee. Then, finally, help us to realize that man was created to shine like stars and live on through all eternity. Keep us, we pray, in perfect peace, help us to walk together, pray together, sing together, and live together until that day when all God's children, Black, White, Red and Yellow will rejoice in one common bank of humanity in the kingdom of our Lord and our God, we pray. Amen.

"Prayer in 1956 by Dr. Martin Luther King, Jr. (1929–1968), the martyred prophet of the Civil Rights Movement, [who] reluctantly accepted leadership of the Montgomery Improvement Association in December 1955 in its effort to desegregate public transportation. Out of his brooding jeremiads, King stubbornly advocated and embraced nonviolent resistance as the best way to depose white supremacy. His spiritual struggles and insights fired the imagination of America." *(Melvin 1994)*

Three

GOSPEL MUSIC DURING THE REBUILDING YEARS

RECORDING ON 45 RPM. By the 1950s, Gospel music in Cleveland forged ahead with tremendous evolutionary strides, influenced largely by the growing popularity of nationally known Gospel groups. The "hard" singing style of the 1950s replaced the softer crooning style of the previous decades. With an improvisational delivery that was altogether wild and audacious, lead singers were known by their unconscious tendencies to slap their thighs while screaming the high notes and were expected to excite and move the audience. Singing live on radio became a thing of the past, Sam Cooke and the Soul Stirrers (nationally known Gospel recording artists during the 1940s) popularized the style of groups singing double lead with four-part harmony, and instruments were used to accompany voice; the "get fiddle," as it was called, and the piano were among the first instruments to be used. Pictured here is the Chariot Gospel Singers' 45 RPM recording of "My Friend" on the Peacock record label. (Image courtesy of Dub Burton.)

THE BRIGHT CLOUDS. This group was organized during the 1950s. Ollie Dotson (back row second from the left) was the manager of the group. (Courtesy of Elizabeth Kinney.)

THE NORTHERN TRAVELERS. Pictured here from front left to right are Jimmy Beverly, William Spanks, Andrew Knuckles, Isaac Talley, Alonzo Pryor, and Andrew Jackson. (Courtesy of Andrew Jackson.)

32

THE ZION STARS. Pictured here are Brother Byrd (holding the guitar), Milton Thomas (front, far right), and Slaughter (back row, center). (Courtesy of Milton Thomas.)

THE FRIENDLY BROTHERS. Under the strong song writing of Bill Spivery (songs such as "Can't Thumb a Ride" and "Operator, Get Me Jesus on the Line"), this group became known throughout the United States during the 1950s and 1960s. Pictured here in the front row from left to right are Amon Jones, Jimmy Morris, and Reverend McDonald. (Courtesy of Virginia Cross.)

THE LEWIS SINGERS. Truly giving praise in this photo, looking up towards heaven with out-stretched hands, the Lewis Singers give you a feeling of total praise. (Courtesy of Marva Bright.)

34

THE UNION STARS. So much in vocal music from the 20th century, including the complete genre of doo wop, is heavily influenced by the vocal harmony set down by early gospel groups like the Union Stars.(Courtesy of Calvin Allen.)

THE SPIRITUAL KINGS. One very important aspect of gospel vocal harmony in groups like the Spiritual Kings is that is was the first music from black america to cross over to the white american audiences. (Courtesy of Elizabeth Kinney.)

THE SPIRITUAL BLENDERS. Ensembles of two to six voices, commonly referred to as "Gospel groups" were everywhere in large numbers during the 1950s. The voices were mixed, but more frequently they were all female generally accompanied by a piano or organ and an occasional percussion instrument. (Courtesy of Virginia Cross.)

THE GOLDEN HARMONETTES. In the year 1959, a group of young Christian women joined together to organize the Temple of Peace Harmonettes (later renamed the Golden Harmonettes) under the leadership of Pastor I.B. Martin, along with Marva Bright and the Carloyn Pettis. After several months, JoAnn Oliver would join this group and become the voice instructor. In 1975, the group sang to a 21,000-crowd audience at Cleveland Municipal Stadium. Pictured here from the front row left to right are Jean Banks, Irene Caesar, and unidentified and in the back row are Marva Bright and JoAnn Oliver. (Courtesy of Marva Bright.)

HENRY BOSSARD. Henry Bossard was known as one of the better bass singers in the country. He left the Swan Silvertones to form the Chariot Gospel Singers of Cleveland. (Courtesy of Charles Smith.)

COMPACT DISC LABEL. This is the cover of a re-issued CD of the Chariot Gospel Singers debut album, which was recorded on the Peacock label. (Courtesy of Charles Smith.)

THE CHARIOT GOSPEL SINGERS ("THE SWEET CHARIOTS"). This group was organized in 1957 by Henry Bossard, a former bass singer with the Swan Silvertones. When the group began, it consisted of the Ensley Jubilees, Floyd Speight, Reverend Charles Williams, Ike Rankins, Ocie Rush, Leonard Dixon, Tommy Cole, Robert Gamble, and Charles Smith on guitar. (Courtesy of Charles Smith.)

THE GOLDEN CROWNS. Pictured in the center is James Malone, the group's guitarist and lead singer. From left to right in the front row are Lee Malone (founder), Floyd Latimore, Charles ?, Leroy Dye, "Slim," and George ?. (Courtesy of Virginia Cross.)

THE MISSIONARY SINGERS. The Missionary Singers was a very popular group during the 1960s. Sister Fingers (back row center) was known for her hard lead vocals on songs like "Something Got a Hold On Me," "I'm Too Close to Heaven, I Can't Turn Around," and "Walk Around My Bedside Lord." Mrs. Dean (front row right) was known for her occasional squall (a harmonic holler). (Courtesy of Marva Bright.)

THE THOMAS BROTHERS. This picture of the Thomas Brothers was taken in the 1950s. (Courtesy of Alex Thomas.)

THE SILVER CHIMES. This picture of the Silver Chimes includes members who were added after the original group was organized. Pictured from left to right are Brenda M. Ware-Abrams, Ann Dudley, Fannie Lucas, Eloise McClarty, and Juanita Crider. (Courtesy of Marva Bright.)

THE GOLDEN CROWNS. This group was founded by lead singer Lee Malone. They sought style and perfection in everything that they did. (Courtesy of Virginia Cross.)

TRUMPETS OF JOY. This picture of the Trumpets of Joy was likely taken in the 1960s. (Courtesy of Mona Boyd.)

THE WONDER TONES. This picture is believed to have been taken in the 1950s. (Courtesy of James Blackwell.)

THE OHIO SPIRITUALS. Formed in 1957 by Sarah Scott, members of the group pictured here from left to right (front row) are unidentified, Judy Carter, Verneda Smith, unidentified, and Elizabeth Kinney. (Courtesy of Elizabeth Kinney.)

THE WOMACK BROTHERS. This family group, which consisted of a father and his five sons, was a well-known Gospel group in and around Cleveland during the 1960s. Pictured here in the front row from left to right are Franky Womack, Franky Womack, Jr., Cecil Womack, Bobby Womack, Curtis Womack, and Harry James Womack. Bobby Womack went on in the 1970s and 1980s to be a national recording R&B singer. (Courtesy of Eloise Burnett.)

THE GLOVER SPECIALS. This family group began singing together in the 1960s. E.B. Glover, father of the group, is seated here with his guitar. Other members of the group from left to right are Robert Glover, unidentified, Ada Glover (mother of the group), Willie Glover, and Shirley Glover. Mr. Glover previously sang with the L&N Singers. (Courtesy of Robert Glover.)

Four

GOSPEL MUSIC DURING THE STRUGGLE FOR CIVIL RIGHTS

HOUGH RIOTS OF 1966. This photograph was taken during the infamous Cleveland Hough Riots of 1966 at the intersection of Addison and Superior Roads. Outside of the Astor Theatre, people were gathered in the momentary calm. Like the rest of our nation, Clevelanders were deeply affected by racial tension, unemployment, and the assassinations of Martin Luther King, Jr. and Malcolm X, and riots were one of the manifestations of these feelings of pain and frustration. Gospel music was instrumental in restoring peace in the black community. It is interesting to note that the Astor Theatre pictured here was converted into a house of praise and worship as the home of the Original Glorious Church Convention Center where countless Gospel quartet programs have been held. (Courtesy of the Cleveland Public Library.)

THE CLEVELAND ALL STARS. Members of the Cleveland All Stars migrated from the Thomas Brothers. They are pictured here around 1961. (Courtesy of Alex Thomas.)

THE FRIENDLY BROTHERS. The Friendly Brothers was a very popular group. Lead singers Bill Spivery (front center) and Jimmy Morris (front left of center) are pictured here. (Courtesy of Virginia Cross.)

48

THE CANAANITES. The Black Renaissance had some early influence on the way of singing and interpreting negro spirituals. First, the historical meaning of these songs were put forward. Then, singers were pushed to be more educated. (Courtesy of Virginia Cross.)

THE CHOSEN CONSOLATORS. In 1963, four former members of the Golden Echoes, Lawrence Thomas, Val Watson, Lee Booker, and Roosevelt Miller, decided to blend their voices in song. Out of this experiment came another group of the 1960s—the Chosen Consolators. Added later were members Eddie Witmore, Milton Graham, and Jesse Fisher. (Courtesy of Marva Bright.)

THE SONS OF TRUTH. Bill Spivery and Jimmy Jones led this group of extraordinary gentlemen throughout the 1960s and 1970s. "Operator Get Me Jesus on the Line" and "How Great Thou Are" are just two of the songs they made famous throughout America. (Courtesy of Virginia Cross.)

THE BRIGHT CLOUDS. This group was managed by Ollie Dotson. Pictured here are Ollie Dotson and unidentified in the front and from left to right are Jeter, Deacon Harris, Ervin Evens, Simon, Tommy Adams. (Courtesy of Virginia Cross.)

THE FRIENDLY SEVEN. This group was first organized in the early 1960s by Macie Maynard as the C.T. Specials. Pictured here from left to right are Mary Haynes (seated at the piano), Reverend Phillip Brown, Rosemary Moore, Betty Thompson, Cherry Pack, and Mr. Eugene Bullock (Vergie Bradford, also part of the group, is not shown here). Their style was very jubilant in the traditional Gospel sound with rich piano and the energetic lead vocals of Betty. (Courtesy of Mary Haynes.)

THE CLEVELAND ALL STARS. This picture is believed to have been taken in the 1960s. Pictured here from the front left to right are Joe Pearson, Leonard Nicholson, Bob ?, A.J. ?, Floyd Latimore, Mr. Burnett, and Chuck Stanberry. (Courtesy of Papa Joe.)

SWANEE NIGHTINGALES.
Members pictured here
from left to right are
Wesley Mitchell, Lamar ?,
Willie Drake, Cary Mitchell,
Tommy White, and
unidentified. (Courtesy
of Cary Mitchell.)

THE GOLDEN HARMONIZERS. Members of the Golden Harmonizers pictured here from left to right are John Smith, unidentified, Eddie Rodgers, Reverend Andrew Smith, and William Durer. (Courtesy of Ann Dudley.)

SONS OF HARMONY. Reverend David Watts is pictured here in the center. (Courtesy of David Watts.)

THE SOUL TOUCHERS. Here is a picture of the Soul Touchers taken during the 1960s. (Courtesy of Ann Dudley.)

★ WORLD-FAMOUS ★
APOLLO
IN THE HEART OF FRIENDLY HARLEM!
★★★★★★★ 125th ST. near 8th Ave. • Tele. UNiversity 4-4490 ★★★★★

TEN DAYS
BEGINNING
FRIDAY
JULY 12th

WADO'S

JOE CRANE
PRESENTS
GOSPEL

"MEETING TONITE"   "GOD IS REAL"

THE **SWANEE** QUINTET

JAMES CLEVELAND

"THE LOVE OF GOD"   AND THE **GOSPEL CHIMES**

"HOW GREAT THOU ART"

THE **HARMONIZING** FOUR

"I WILL TRUST IN THE LORD"

PROF. **CHARLES TAYLOR** SINGERS

"NEAR THE CROSS"

ARCO SINGERS

THE
CONSOLERS
"EVERY CHRISTIANIOTHER"

THE **SINGING**
"NOW MY LORD"
CRUSADERS

GOSPEL MUSIC POSTER. Ten days of Gospel singing! This poster advertised a concert featuring the hottest groups in the nation at that time, including Cleveland's own the "Singing Crusaders." (Courtesy of Howard Sharp.)

THE SINGING CRUSADERS. The Singing Crusaders was organized in 1961 at the home of Eugene Hall. The group consisted of Howard Sharp, Jr., Robert L. Fields, Jimmy Thomas, Baby George Smith, H. Sweeny, R. Ezell, Eugene Hall, C. Grant, and A. Bell. (Courtesy of Howard Sharp.)

THE SINGING CRUSADERS. This picture of the Singing Crusaders was taken during their performance at the Apollo Theatre in Harlem, New York in 1963. This concert was promoted by Doc Joe Crane of WADO Radio for a ten-day performance. (Courtesy of Howard Sharp.)

THE SEVEN REVELATORS. Pictured here from left to right are F. Blue, F. Green, Mildred Jones, Hattie Osborne, Lula Nicks, and E. J. Nicks. (Courtesy of Marva Bright.)

THE GOLDEN HARMONETTES. Pictured here from the front left to right are Jean Banks (seated), JoAnn Oliver, Velma Peoples, Ann Killings, Phyliss Jackson, and Marva Bright. (Courtesy of Marva Bright.)

THE REVELATORS. The Revelators were a local favorite with their harmony and stage performance. (Courtesy of Marva Bright.)

THE CHERUBIMS. This group was organized in 1957 by Gloria Hardy and Barbara Kelly. Reverend Easter Smith gave them their name. It's been said that the group was 20 years ahead of their time. Their jazz chord harmonies were a first for Gospel groups. The group has recorded three 45 RPM records and two albums. (Courtesy of Barbara Kelly.)

THE SENSATIONAL SAINTS. This group was well known for their vocal harmony. (Courtesy of Virginia Cross.)

THE HARPETTES. Under the leadership of Barbara Irving and Barbara Boone, this group was well known for their dedication, sacrifice, and contributions to the city of Cleveland. This group still sings today under the leadership of Reverend Boone. (Courtesy of Reverend Esqulaira LeSure.)

STARS OF HARMONY. Under the leadership of Robert Reynolds, this publicity photo of the Stars of Harmony show how the groups of that time used their creativity and design skills to set them apart from the other gospel groups. (Courtesy of Robert Reynolds.)

JUBILEE SPECIALS OF WARREN, OHIO. While this group did not originate in the greater Cleveland area, it was well known in and around Cleveland as a Boddie recording artist. (Courtesy of Thomas Boddie.)

RECORDING ON 45 RPM. This is an image of the Cleveland Golden Echoes' recording of "For 30 Pieces of Silver" on the Bounty record label. It was recorded in 1974. (Courtesy of Dub Burton.)

THE MORNING STARS. Pictured here is Brother Gibson (center, holding the mic). (Courtesy of Sister Obey.)

THE WONDERS OF FAITH. This family group included mother Mary Johnson and daughters Freda, Eloise, and Bobbie, along with family friend Mary Caldwell. This group had a strong presence in the 1960s. (Courtesy of Mary Caldwell.)

LITTLE ROCK BAPTIST CHURCH. During the 1970s, this church was home to many Gospel concerts. (Courtesy of Frederick Burton.)

THE MASTER KEYS. In 1963, the original members of the Master Keys were David LeSure, Johnny Haymon, John Jackson, Herbert Davidson, Samuel Fisher, and Hubert Vaden. The group recorded their first record in the year of their formation with a record company in New York. The Master Keys still sing today and celebrated their 43rd anniversary in June 2003. Dub Burton joined the group in 1965 and remains a member today. Pictured here from left to right are Johnny Haymon, Dub Burton, John Crockett, Wesley Woods, Hubert Vaden, Gene Griffin, Arthur Pack, and John Jackson. (Courtesy of Dub Burton.)

GOSPEL SINGING AWARD. The Master Keys received this award in 1964 from the Gospel *Singers Journal* for the tenth most popular group in Cleveland. (Courtesy of Dub Burton.)

THE MAJESTIC HOTEL RESTAURANT. In the 1960s, the restaurant inside the Majestic Hotel, located at East Fifty-Fifth and Central, was owned and operated by Skippy and Odessa Still. It was a frequent dining spot for Cleveland Gospel singers and their out-of-town guests. (Courtesy of Marva Bright.)

THE SILVER KINGS. L.A. Valentine (kneeling in front on the right) was a talented lead vocalist who became well known for the "call and response." (Courtesy of Elizabeth Kinney.)

SPIRITUAL FOUR. While many quartets were literal quartets, the term became used to describe the style of small group singing, rather than the actual number of singers. (Courtesy of Elizabeth Kinney.)

THE ANGELIC SINGERS. At church, hymns and psalms were sung during services. Some of them were transformed into songs of a typical African-American form: they are "Dr. Watts." The lyrics of negro spirituals were tightly linked with the lives of their authors, who were slaves. While work songs dealt only with their daily life, spirituals were inspired by the message. (Courtesy of Marva Bright.)

THE MUNNDORA'S SINGERS. This family group was founded by their father, Deacon Munn of Prince of Peace Baptist Church. (Courtesy of Mona Boyd.)

THE UNION STARS AS THEY APPEARED IN THE 1960s. Primarily, performers have shaped the basic styles of gospel music, individually and collectively. Because of the highly improvisatory nature of gospel music, the composers of many gospel songs are never known. (Courtesy of Calvin Alvin.)

THE MIGHTY RIGHTEOUS SOULS.
Jesse Lavendar (front row on
left) is the lead singer of this
famed quartet group famous for
"Let Me Lean on You" and "Lord
I Know You've Been So Good."
(Courtesy of Jesse Lavendar.)

THE HEAVENLY WONDERS. The Heavenly Wonders was a group far ahead of their time. They had great appearance, musical sound, and vocals. Reverend Johnny Twymon, pastor of the Blessed Hope Missionary Baptist Church, is pictured here on the far right. (Courtesy of Reverend Johnny Twymon.)

69

THE GOSPEL HEBREWS. Pictured here in a 1960s photograph from the front left to right are Dave Harris, Willie Ezell, Andrew Jackson, Frank ?, Thomas ?, and Singer Chappell. (Courtesy of Minnie Ezell.)

SOUL TOUCHERS. The Soul Touchers were Boddie recording artists. Reverend McDonald (holding the guitar) was a pioneer guitar player. (Courtesy of Ann Dudley.)

The Fourth Anniversary

of The Magnificent Soul Touchers

at ST. MATTHEW METHODIST CHURCH
1516 E. 86th Street

SUNDAY, DECEMBER 1st, 1968, 8 p. m.

Featuring: Elite Jewels - Sensational Saints
Mid-South Gospel Singers of Detroit, Mich

Advance $1.25   Door $1.50

Rev. Clemmons, Pastor   W. McDonald, Mgr

GOSPEL CONCERT ADMISSION TICKET. This ticket was for admission to the Soul Touchers fourth anniversary held in Cleveland in 1968. (Courtesy of Ann Dudley.)

CELESTIAL COETS. The early Gospel choirs were often groups varying in size and mixed voices, singing traditional Gospel hymns in Gospel style—usually syncopated versions of these well-known hymn tunes. As the Gospel choir took on commercial appeal after the pattern of the Wings over Jordan group, more attention was devoted to the development of a unique and original sound, like the Celestial Coets pictured here. (Courtesy of Thomas Boddie.)

Five

GOSPEL MUSIC DURING THE RESURGENT YEARS

ST. MATTHEWS METHODIST CHURCH. This church was the site of many Gospel music concerts during the 1960s and 1970s. The vast majority of the Cleveland quartet groups did not go "on the road" (a term referring to paid professional singers). Rather than seeking fame and fortune at the expense of their good paying jobs at local factories like the Ford Motor Company and Republic Steel, many quartet singers were content to travel on weekends and do summer tours and perform at local churches and auditoriums. (Courtesy of Frederick Burton.)

THE SENSATIONAL SAINTS. This group became a national recording artist and one of the most popular and well-respected groups in Cleveland. (Courtesy of Ray Kennibrew.)

THE FANTASTIC SPIRITUAL BELIEVERS. This group was organized in 1970. It was the prayers of this dynamic quartet that their many songs of worship illuminate as well as edify both the mind and the spirit of all God's children. (Courtesy of Thomas Boddie.)

THE MODERNAIRS. Pictured here from the top left to right are Burge, Lawrence, Bridges (center), Milton, and Streeter. (Courtesy of Reverend Esqulaira LeSure.)

THE RUFFIN SINGERS. This group was one of the first family groups to emerge on the scene in the 1970s. Managed by father Jerry Ruffin, Sr., their performances were always spirit-filled and the audience assured to be blessed. (Courtesy of Dub Burton.)

THE LOCKETT SINGERS. Brother Charles Dixon of the Gospel Hi-Risers appears here with the Lockett Singers in front of Aunt Tailor's House in Chicago on April 17, 1977. (Courtesy of Sister Lockett.)

SOUNDS OF SOUL. This group began singing together in 1975 under the leadership of A.J. Thomas. Original members were Ben Davis, Leonard Foster, Milton Bridges, John Studemire (front center), and Roosevelt Ezell. (Courtesy of Roosevelt Ezell.)

SWANEE NIGHTINGALES. Here is a 1970s picture of the Swanee Nightingales in front of Triedstone Baptist Church. (Courtesy of Reverend Esqulaira LeSure.)

THE BURTON SINGERS. The Burton Singers was a family group that began singing together in 1971. The group included father Dub Burton and his four children, Frederick, Derlein, Zebra, and Roderick. Nephew Tony Nick Baker and cousin Angie Elmore also were among the original members of the group. Pictured here from left to right in the front row are Dub Burton, Zebra Burton Rice, Roderick Burton, Tony Nick Baker, Derlein Burton Means, and Frederick Burton. (Courtesy Dub Burton.)

THE JOYNETTES. Deacon Savage managed this group. Laura Pointer appears in the back row center, and Georgia is to her right. (Courtesy of Reverend Esqulaira LeSure.)

THE GOLDEN HARMONETTES. This picture of the Golden Harmonettes was taken in the 1970s. Pictured here from left to right in the front row are Ann Killings and JoAnn Oliver, and in the back row are Velma Peoples, Betty McDonald, Marva Bright, Flo Jackson, and Bessie Henderson. (Courtesy of Marva Bright.)

THE GOSPEL CHOSEN FEW. Pictured here in tuxedos, this group emerged in the 1970s. Cary Mitchell, lead singer and manager of the group, is standing on the far left. (Courtesy of Cary Mitchell.).

YOUR ALTERNATIVE, A CHRISTIAN NIGHT CLUB. Once the Kinsman Grill owned by Sonny Jones, a hot spot for secular entertainment, Your Alternative was converted into a popular Christian nightclub—the first of its kind in Cleveland. Pictured here in song in 1985 from left to right are Derlein Burton Means, Dub Burton, Felice Harriston, and Debbie Baker of the Burton Singers. After closing its doors as a Christian night club, Your Alternative became the first location of the Blessed Hope Missionary Baptist Church. (Courtesy of Dub Burton.)

THE GOLDEN HARMONETTES. Here are the Golden Harmonettes in a performance at the Cleveland Stadium. (Courtesy of Marva Bright.)

THE GOLDEN HARMONIZERS. This is a picture of the Golden Harmonizers as they appeared in the 1970s. (Courtesy of Marva Bright.)

THE SAINTS OF GLORY. Pictured here from the front left to right are Greg Harris, Wayne ?, Richard Harris, Lucky ?, unidentified, Ben Block, and Slaughter. (Courtesy of Elizabeth Kinney.)

THE GOSPEL HEBREWS. This is a picture of the Gospel Hebrews as they appeared in the 1980s. From left to right are Rick Harris, Dave Harris, Frank, and Sandy Harris. (Courtesy of Marva Bright.)

THE HAYMON SINGERS. In 1970, the Haymon Singers were organized by the father of the group, Johnny Haymon, who is also one of the original members of the Master Keys. The original members included children Jose, Jackie, Reginald, Myra, Sabrina, and Paul and nephew Floyd Haymon. With no formal training, the musicians in the group were self-taught. Paul's rhythmic beats on the drums and Myra's accomplishments on the bass distinguished this young family group in the 1970s. (Courtesy of Johnny Haymon.)

THE GOSPEL PEARLS. Members of the Gospel Pearls pictured here in front from left to right are Bell, Gail, Candy, Nadine, Genethia, and Helen. (Courtesy of Bell.)

THE WATCHINGAIRES. The Watchingaires appear here just prior to a Gospel concert. The corsages they are wearing suggest that this concert was in celebration of their anniversary. (Courtesy of Sister Lockett.)

THE NEW BRIGHT CLOUDS. This picture of the New Bright Clouds shows the dramatic change in dress and hairstyle that was prevalent in the 1970s. (Courtesy of Tommy Adams.)

THE MIGHTY RIGHTEOUS SOULS. This is a more recent photo of the Mighty Righteous Souls. Although a little older, their song ministry continued to be spirit-filled and effective. (Courtesy of Jesse Lavendar.)

THE CHRISTIAN BROTHERS. David LeSure, Sr. (far left), father of this family group, is shown here singing the group's popular favorite "Drippin' and Droppin'." Also pictured from left to right are Reverend Esqulaira LeSure (in back, playing the lead guitar), Darrell Harriston (at the mic), Chuck Stanberry (in back, playing the bass guitar), Jimmy Gray (at the mic), and David LeSure, Jr. (at the mic on far right). (Courtesy of Derlein Means.)

THE NEW HEAVENLY WONDERS OF THE 1970s. Pictured here in front from left to right are Hank, Ronnie, and Roscoe, and in the back from left to right are Frank, Jr., Bill, Orthello, and Reverend Twymon. (Courtesy of Reverend Twymon.)

THE LORETTAETTES. The Lorettaettes are pictured here in concert at a local church. (Courtesy of Mona Boyd.)

THE SPIRITUAL FIVE. With traditional songs and sweet harmony, this family group epitomized the Christian quartet groups of old. Willie Yarborough, Sr., along with his sons, started what came to be known as the "Cancer Gospelthon," an all-day Gospel concert, the proceeds of which were donated to the American Cancer Society. (Courtesy of the Thomas Singers.)

THE MACK SINGERS. The Mack Singers was organized by the father of the group, Bobby McCafferty (far left). One of their more popular songs was "Down on My Knees." Daughter Valerie (left at the mic) was an incredible lead soprano with a spirited, natural high voice that granted her unbelievable range. The group also included daughters Theresa (center) and Pamela (right). Other members at different times included Vanessa Ford-Williams, Beverly Ford, Lisa Ford, Danise Haynes, Bryan McCafferty, Diana Turner, and Gloria Stokes. (Courtesy of the Burton Singers.)

THE GOSPEL TRAVELERS. Often called the "young gents of Gospel" by emcee Larry Dominic, this group is pictured here singing at Consolation. Members of the group pictured from front left to right are Chuck Tyree, Demetrius Moore, and Dwayne "Sonny" Banks. (Courtesy of the Burton Singers.)

THE GOSPEL HI-RISERS. This is a picture of another very talented singing group. They are best remembered for the smooth falsetto of the father and lead singer of the group. (Courtesy of Mrs. Dixon.)

THE SEVEN REVELATORS. Appearing here at a concert in Detroit, Michigan in 1981 are the Seven Revelators. Sister Scales is standing in the front with her back to the audience. (Courtesy of Margaret Scales.)

THE GOLDEN ECHOES. The Golden Echoes are pictured here in the 1980s. (Courtesy of Barbara Kelly.)

THE SPIRITUAL BELIEVERS. Taken in the 1980s, the Spiritual Believers are pictured here in symmetric formation. From left to right are Joe, Val, Walter Glenn, Hubie Vaden, Jimmie Ash, Nathaniel Congress, Simon Congress, and Leonard Nicholson. (Courtesy of Marva Bright.)

MICHAEL FISHER. This is a picture of Michael Fisher, lead singer of the Gospel Travelers. (Courtesy of Derlein Means.)

THE L&N GOSPEL SINGERS. This picture was taken in the 1970s and includes E.B. Glover (in front) and Robert Glover (standing at the right). (Courtesy of Robert Glover.)

THE OPERATORS. This group was organized in 1977 by Bill Spivery. The group recorded its first album in November 1977, with the Savoy Record Company of Elizabeth, New Jersey and entitled it "Trouble With the Operator." They traveled throughout the U.S. singing God's praises. Favorite songs were "I Surrender All," "I'm Glad To Be In the Church," and "Get Out of the Way." Pictured here from left to right are Missionary Jenny Powell, Barbara Carr, Marva Bright, Bill Spivery, and Doris Workman. (Courtesy of Marva Bright.)

THE ROYAL JUBILEE SINGERS. This group started as a trio in the basement of Freeman Mays with Joe Campbell and Singer Chappell, the group's founder. Under Chappell's leadership, they became organized and known in the Gospel singers' community. Other singers were added: Nathaniel Williams, Reverend Archie Moore, Leroy Jackson, Milton Thomas, Reverend Milton Bridges, Sr., Milton Bridges, Jr., and Lawrence Williams. (Courtesy of Milton Thomas.)

THE PRINCE OF PEACE ENSEMBLE. Members Terry, Scumby, Anthony, and John relax before they are scheduled to sing. (Courtesy of Mona Boyd.)

THE BURTON SINGERS. Taken in 1983, the Burton singers had become well respected for their spirit-filled presence and stage performances. Although varying interests among the group led to their separation in 1985, after 13 years of singing great Gospel music, the group has reunited on special occasions to sing. Pictured here from left to right in the front row are Felice Harriston, Debbie Baker, Derlein Burton Means, Dub Burton, Tony Nick Baker, Frederick Burton, Roderick Burton, and Troy Henderson. (Courtesy of Dub Burton.)

THE SUPREME ANGELS. Founded by Walter Deadwyler, the lead singer and bass player, the Supreme Angels featured his son's lead guitar solos and the drum solos of his daughter. (Courtesy of Walter Deadwyler.)

THE NEW HEAVENLY WONDERS. There has to be a commitment to hold a group together. Over the years, many of the groups that had longevity were forced to adjust to sustain, but the style and sound remained the same. This picture illustrates the transformation of the New Heavenly Wonders from an all male group to a male-female group. Pictured in front from left to right are Danise Willis, Shryle Perkins, and Logan Bean, and in the second row from left to right are Leon Fields, Gail Twymon, Gloria Stokes, and Reverend Twymon, and in the back row from left to right are Orthello Bell, Reverend Larry Perkins, and Dianne Turner. (Courtesy of Reverend Twymon.)

PROFESSOR RILEY AND THE HARMONY THREE PLUS. Professor Riley (top center) was a well-respected music director who led many groups and choirs in singing Gospel music. (Courtesy of Brenda M. Ware-Abrams.)

THE SENSATIONAL SAINTS. Reverend Melvin Kennibrew is pictured here with the Sensational Saints, carrying the ubiquitous white handkerchief as he sings. (Courtesy of Mona Boyd.)

BELLS OF JOY. Sister Obey (seated) organized this group in the 1980s. (Courtesy of Sister Obey.)

THE THOMPSON SINGERS. This group was organized under the direction of Lewis Thompson, Sr. and Willie Yarborough, Sr. of the Spiritual Five Gospel Singers. During the 1980s, the Thompson Singers performed on many "Gospelthons" sponsored by the Spiritual Five. They have performed in and out of the Cleveland area including the Gospel Music Workshop of America. (Courtesy of the Thompson Singers.)

THE NEW HARPETTES. Reverend Boone is pictured here with the New Harpettes. He led the group and was their musician. (Courtesy of The New Harpettes.)

THE SONS OF TRUTH. This group continues to sing God's praises in and around Cleveland. Pictured here with his sons is Alphonso Smith (front left), known by everyone as "Smitty."

THE CHRISTIAN BROTHERS. This is a picture of the successor group of the original Christian Brothers. Pictured here from left to right are Emory Hosea Nash, Ellis Sims, Reverend Lyneil Nash, Reverend Esqulaira LeSure, and Kelvin LeSure, Sr. (Courtesy of Reverend Esqulaira LeSure.)

THE SHIELDS BROTHERS. This is a picture of the Shields Brothers in the 1980s. (Courtesy of Claude Shields, Jr.)

THE MACK SINGERS. Here are members of the Mack Singers at a local Gospel concert. Pictured from left to right are Pam, Linda, Theresa, and Valerie. (Courtesy of Pamela LeSure.)

TURNER FAMILY GOSPEL SINGERS. This is a picture of another family Gospel group. (Courtesy the Turner Family.)

BELLS OF JOY. This candid shot of the Bells of Joy singing features from left to right Ann McCloudy, Katherine Obey, Florine Adams, Evangelist Atkins, and Sue Gibson. (Courtesy of Brenda M. Ware-Abrams.)

Cory United Methodist Church. This local church was the site of many larger Gospel quartet concerts in the 1960s. (Courtesy of Frederick Burton.)

The New Master Keys. Here is a later picture of the New Master Keys. Pictured from left to right are Matthew Lester, Bobby Fuller, Fred Burrse, John Truitt, Dub Burton, and Arthur Pack. (Courtesy of Dub Burton.)

THE SINGERS JOURNAL. This image is of the front cover of the October 1964 edition of the *Singers Journal*, a periodic publication that was sold in and around Cleveland. It highlighted local Gospel talent and provided information on upcoming events and activities. (Courtesy of Marva Bright.)

Six

PROMOTING CLEVELAND'S GOSPEL MUSIC

ON THE AIR. "Turn Your Radio On," sung by national recording artist the Sensational Nightingales, was a popular Gospel song during the 1950s and 1960s. This song graced Arthur Turner's radio broadcast. The radio was the primary vehicle through which Gospel music entered thousands of homes in Cleveland each week. A historical perspective on Gospel music in Cleveland would not be complete without a look at the individuals who promoted local Gospel talent and their music. In their own unique way, radio announcers, music recorders, promoters, and mistresses and masters of ceremonies helped to spread Gospel music through radio broadcasts, Gospel concerts, and musical assemblies. Popularity for Cleveland Gospel music spread beyond Cleveland's greater metropolitan area to many national forums like Chicago, Detroit, New York, Rochester, Birmingham and Jacksonville (Alabama), and St. Louis. Gospel groups from around the country coupled with local talents filled the roster of many Gospel programs in and around Cleveland.

ARTHUR TURNER. Arthur Turner was a well-respected Gospel music promoter who broadcasted on WABQ and WJMO radio stations, beginning a career in broadcasting in 1948. For 52 years, he managed the Elite Jewels, and he was the last original member of the Shields Brothers. He was also one of the founding members of the Ohio Singers Movement and the Gospel Music Workshop of America (Cleveland Chapter). If there was a major Gospel concert coming to town, chances were pretty good that it was being promoted by Arthur Turner. (Courtesy of Willie Mae Reese.)

MARY HOLT. This photograph of Mary Holt, a familiar religious radio announcer, was taken in 1957. (Courtesy of the Cleveland Public Library.)

LEROY GAYNOR WITH ARTHUR TURNER. An imposing stature, LeRoy Gaynor (left), once a promoter, radio announcer, member of the Harmony Echoes, and founding member of the Ohio Gospel Singers Movement, is pictured here with Arthur Turner at a Gospel music concert. (Courtesy of Willie Mae Reese.)

SKIPPY STILL. Skippy Still, with his wife Odessa (below) of 50 years, initially embraced the airwaves of Cleveland and the surrounding areas on the first Sunday in August 1959. They began broadcasting over station WMMS FM, moved to WABQ AM six months later, and ultimately broadcasted together for 15 years on WJMO AM. Through radio ministry, they encouraged the sick and shut-in and informed listeners of community services, activities, and Gospel music events. (Courtesy of Virginia Cross.)

ODESSA STILL. A profound legend in the art of broadcasting, Odessa Still has received local and national recognition. She is known and has earned the title of "queen of the airwaves" among her constituents. She has been a member of the Gospel Music Workshop of America for the past 35 years, a radio announcer for the past 42 years, and she is a humanitarian, Gospel promoter, frequent emcee, mentor, and friend to many. (Courtesy of Odessa Still.)

BILL SPIVERY. Singer, songwriter, arranger, record producer, manager, founder, playwright, and religious announcer are but a few words to describe Bill Spivery. He was an on-air personality in Cleveland for over 40 years, he is an inductee into the Broadcasters Hall of Fame, and he is a founding member of the Gospel Music Workshop of America (Cleveland Chapter). Bill Spivery was the winner of the Midwest Urban Awards for most favorite Gospel radio personality in 1993, and he wrote one of the most popular Gospel songs in the United States to come out of Cleveland—"Operator, Get Me Jesus On the Line." (Courtesy of Bill Spivery.)

THE PLAIN DEALER/ WEDNESDAY, NOVEMBER 17, 1993

TODAY

TV show gets song about JFK new airing

By JANE SCOTT
PLAIN DEALER ROCK REPORTER

CLEVELAND

Ask not of your country what it can do for you/ Ask of your country what would it have you do/ With those famous words the world has lost a friend/ But the strange thing about his life/ It seems it never ends.
-- From "Mr. John," Tahoe/London Records, 1964.

Songwriter/gospel singer Bill Spivery surely will be watching "Jack," tonight's CBS two-hour documentary on John F. Kennedy (9 p.m., WJW Channel 8) with more than just a cursory interest.

His folk song, "Mr. John," will be the last notes on the film, which includes narrations by the late president, his family and colleagues. "Mr. John" stands out from other songs on the program because it is played as the credits roll, with no picture distractions.

"Can you imagine? After 30 years! I wrote that song from my heart, just a little after he was shot," says Spivery, 62, a Saturday afternoon disc jockey on WABQ-AM/1540. "I thought so much of President Kennedy. I was on welfare then, working maintenance at the CMHA project on Cedar-Central. The words just came to me while I was working."

Cleveland singer Bobby Womack encouraged Spivery to record his words. So Spivery took his guitarist cousin,

he got songwriter Jimmy Testa to help with it."

Testa put the "real flavor" into the song, arranged it and played guitar on it down at Cleveland Recording on Feb. 12, 1964.

"And it was a wonderful session," said engineer Ken Hamann, now president of Suma Recording Studio. "We did the song in two or three takes. Bill had a bunch of kids down here with him to sing the 'Mr. John' and 'Mr. Kennedy' chorus. I've still got the mas-

London Records. Maduri and firms, Miss Area! Music and T sic, respectively, have the pu rights.

"That was my beginning. I welfare and went on to wri songs," says Spivery. Twelve ye he made news when his "O song was a big hit for the Mi Transfer.

"Mr. John" never became a hit. "Broadcasters absolutely not to play songs written af Kennedy tragedy in respect to

Bill Spivery, left, holds a copy of his record, "Mr. John." Jimmy Testa his guitar. Engineer Ken Hamann is at right.

NEWS ARTICLE. This is an image of a *Cleveland Plain Dealer* newspaper article on Bill Spivery's song "Mr. John," which was written about President John F. Kennedy. Spivery received national recognition for the song, which rose on the record charts in Cleveland to number three. (Courtesy of Bill Spivery.)

KEN HAWKINS. Ken Hawkins was a radio disc jockey and program director of WJMO who promoted live Gospel singing on the air during the 1960s. (Courtesy of Cleveland Public Library.)

FAIR PROMOTERS CLUB. An organized group for the promotion of Gospel music in Cleveland, the Fair Promoters Club was organized by William "Skippy" Still, Odessa Still, Woody Coleman, and Ester Neal on July 7, 1958. The Club promoted such groups as the Highway QCs, Staple Singers, James Cleveland, Swan Silvertones, Blind Boys, and the Mighty Clouds of Joy. (Courtesy of Virginia Cross.)

AT THE RADIO STATION. Pictured here from left to right are Brenda M. Ware-Abrams, Judy Carter, and Lillian Torrence taking calls at WABQ AM radio. These ladies made up a group founded by Odessa Still called The Ladies of Gospel. (Courtesy of Lillian.)

LARRY DOMINIC. For decades, Larry Dominic (better known as "Mr. Personality") was a very familiar on-air radio personality and frequent patron of local Gospel concerts. As a Master of Ceremonies, his famous handle, "I don't know what you come to do, but I come to praise His name," became his trademark. Larry was also a religious announcer for WABQ radio in Cleveland with the "Good News" broadcast. He was a member of the original Ladies & Gents of Gospel. (Courtesy of Brenda M. Ware-Abrams.)

DENVER C. WILBORN. Pictured here in the 1960s, Denver Wilborn was an up and coming Gospel radio announcer employed by WABQ radio. He would quickly be elevated to program director and general operations manager in charge of all airtime content. He was responsible for writing ads and station breaks, selling airtime, hiring, and training radio announcers and other personnel and everything in between. Wilborn was a frequent Master of Ceremonies for local Gospel programs and he managed and was a member of the Angels of Harmony in the 1940s.

BERTHA NOLIN. Bertha Nolin was a secretary to the publishers of the *Singers Journal*, a monthly newsletter distributed in the Gospel singers' market. (Courtesy of Marva Bright.)

REVEREND DAVID WATTS. Reverend Watts is the current pastor of The Greater New Canaan Baptist Church. Being a former quartet singer himself, Reverend Watts has graciously opened the doors of his church to host many Gospel concerts and events. He is pictured here with three members of his congregation. (Courtesy of Mona Boyd.)

DENVER WILBORN AND BRENDA M. WARE-ABRAMS. This picture was taken in 1996 at the induction ceremony of the National Broadcaster's Hall of Fame, where Brenda M. Ware-Abrams was the first Black female announcer from Cleveland to be inducted into the Hall of Fame. (Courtesy of Brenda M. Ware-Abrams.)

THE STATE OF OHIO

E0519-1851

DEPARTMENT OF STATE

TED W. BROWN
Secretary of State

Certificate

411494

It is hereby Certified that the Secretary of State of Ohio has custody of the

Records of Incorporation and Miscellaneous Filings; that said records show

the filing and recording of: __REN AGS__ OF

OHIO SINGERS MOVEMENT

United States of America
STATE OF OHIO
Office of the Secretary of State

Recorded on Roll __E519__ at Frame __1852__ of the

Records of Incorporation and Miscellaneous Filings.

Witness my hand and the seal of the Secretary of State, at the City of

Columbus, Ohio, this __11TH__ day of __DECEMBER__, A.D. 19 __78__

TED W. BROWN

THE OHIO SINGERS MOVEMENT CHARTER. The Ohio Singers Movement received their charter on May 14, 1971. The organization's purpose, among other things, was to assist Gospel promoters and singing groups in calendaring events in and around Cleveland. Founding members included LeRoy Gaynor, Charles Chamblier, Andrew Jackson, and Arthur Turner. (Courtesy of Brenda M. Ware-Abrams.)

HILDA SANFORD. Gospel promoter and supporter best describe a few of the many attributes of Hilda Sanford. While a strong advocate of promoting local talent, she was credited with bringing major Gospel performers into Cleveland. She was also the founder of Dynamic Promotions, a Cleveland-based Gospel music promotion company that was organized in 1963 with Hilda Sanford, Sam Fisher, and John Crockett. Later members included Ann Dudley, Mary McCoy, Dolores Vaden, and Mary Williams. (Courtesy of Brenda M. Ware-Abrams.)

DOLORES VADEN. Miss Dee, as her friends affectionately call her, is another one of Cleveland's fine Gospel promoters. (Courtesy of Brenda M. Ware-Abrams.)

BRO. LEROY GAYN[...]

ON RADIO STATIO[...]
W J M O EACH SU[...]
from 8:30 - 9:3[...]

Mr. Gaynor is a[...]
one of the firs[...]
promoters of th[...]
Singers Journal[...]

WJMO
CLEVELAND 6, OHIO
1490 KC

LISTEN TO:
SATURDAY NIGHT
SPIRITUALS.

Sat. 8: to 9:00 P.M.

The Elite Jewels

Sun. 9:45-10:15 A. M.

SUNDAY SPIRITUALS

10:15 ---- 10:45 A.M.

WJMO Radio Station Promotion. This flier was used to promote a Gospel music broadcast on WJMO radio station in October 1965. (Courtesy of Marva Bright.)

DENVER WILBORN AND FREDDIE BROWN. Denver Wilborn (left) is pictured here with Freddie Brown, pastor of the New Galilee Baptist Church and former lead singer of the Golden Echoes, at a Gospel music concert. (Courtesy of Denver Wilborn.)

ON THE AIR AT WABQ. Dub Burton is pictured in back at the controls at WABQ radio in an on-air broadcast during the 1980s. In addition to founding and managing the Burton Singers Gospel group, he is a Gospel music promoter and is a member of the Ohio Gospel Quartets (Cleveland chapter). (Courtesy of Dub Burton.)

THE FIRST ANNIVERSARY

O F

THE FAIR PROMOTERS

SUNDAY, JULY 10th, 1960

"ALL THINGS WORK TOGETHER FOR GOOD TO
THEM THAT LOVE GOD"—Romans 8:28

FAIR PROMOTERS CLUB. This is the program cover for the Fair Promoters Club's first anniversary (1960). (Courtesy of Virginia Cross.)

BODDIE RECORDING COMPANY, INC. Thomas Boddie (pictured above left) incorporated the Boddie Recording Company in 1973. It is Cleveland's oldest licensed, Black owned recording company, recording under the labels of "Soul Kitchen," "Plaid," "Bounty," and "Lu Au." A 1942 graduate of East Technical High School in Cleveland studying electronics, Boddie went on to become a recording pioneer, and in 1957, recorded his first Gospel artist, the Pronoun Gospel Singers of Flint, Michigan, from the basement of his home. He recorded numerous Cleveland groups as well. In 1975, Boddie was inducted into the Audio Engineers' Society of America. In 1980, Thomas and wife Louise (pictured with Boddie below) expanded their business into on-site video and audio duplication. (Courtesy of Thomas Boddie.)

REVEREND ROBERT LEE PEACOCK, SR. Reverend Robert Lee Peacock, Sr. was known as "the singers' photographer." For the past 30 years, he has skillfully photographed many of the Gospel groups appearing in this book. In 1971, Peacock accepted a calling to preach the Gospel and is now pastor of the Jericho Missionary Baptist Church. (Courtesy of Reverend Robert Lee Peacock, Sr.)

BRENDA M. WARE-ABRAMS. Always cheerful and smiling, Brenda Ware-Abrams is pictured here in the style and elegance that she has come to embody as a religious announcer on WABQ radio station. Since her introduction to Cleveland radio in 1974, Ware-Abrams has been recognized by many organizations and has been a frequent mistress of ceremonies, event speaker, and religious columnist. She is well known for her dedication to community service. (Courtesy of Brenda M. Ware-Abrams.)

LOOK WHO'S COMMING TO TOWN!

GOSPEL HEAVEYWEIGHTS   ELITE JEWELS   HARPETT GOSPEL SINGER

ST. JUDE CHURCH IS PRESENTING
A BIG MUSICAL PROGRAM
——— FEATURING ———

- THE POPULAR GOSPEL HEAVEYWEIGHTS - BROOKLYN, N.Y.
- THE ELITE JEWELS OF CLEVELAND, OHIO
- THE MT. NEBO BAPTIST CHURCH MALE CHROUS
- THE HARPETT GOSPEL SINGERS OF CLEVELAND OHIO

AT JERICHO BAPTIST CHURCH 11918 KINSMAN ROAD
MONDAY JUNE 6, 1977 AT 7:30 P.M.

DONATION $3⁰⁰ ADV. $3⁵⁰ AT THE DOOR

TICKETS ARE AT BENNIES RECORD & VARIETY MART
14701 EUCLID AVE. BEN'S SERVICE STATION
E. 79TH ST. & CEDAR AVE. MUSIC SHACK 9300 WADE PARK AVE
IN MARTIN LUTHER KING PLAZA.

GOSPEL MUSIC FLIER. Fliers such as this one were widely used by Gospel groups to promote upcoming Gospel concerts in the community. (Courtesy of Reverend Esqulaira LeSure.)

GOSPEL RADIO BROADCAST. Pictured here are Reverend Anderson (left) and Evangelist Johnson on the air at WERE radio. (Courtesy of Brenda M. Ware-Abrams.)

KIM FERGUSON AND LOIS SWANSON. Kim Ferguson and Lois Swanson are radio personalities for WABQ radio. They are pictured here at a Gospel program. (Courtesy of Mona Boyd.)

THE SHIELDS BROTHERS. Claude Shields, Jr. (far left) and David Watts (second from the left) appear here outside a Gospel quartet conference. (Courtesy of Claude Shields, Jr.)

AWARDS BANQUET. Reverend Melvin Kennibrew appears here at an awards banquet in recognition of Gospel music accomplishments. (Courtesy of Brenda M. Ware-Abrams.)

SPECIAL
ACKNOWLEDGMENTS

I owe a great deal of thanks to many people for the production of this book. Regennia N. Williams, Ph.D., author, and faculty member in the Department of History at Cleveland State University, was a source of inspiration and encouragement; my father, Dub Burton, was an invaluable source of information and a tremendous aide; and my wife, Benita, worked diligently along my side. This collection would not exist without some very special friends who so graciously loaned their precious memories, time, and counsel. Listed below are those individuals who contributed in a special way, along with the names of the groups, radio announcers, and promoters who appear in this collection.

Contributors

Ascension
Ollie Billings
Thomas Boddie
Eloise Burnett
Benita Burton
Dub Burton
Yvonne Burton
Mona Boyd
Marva Bright
John Chappell
Virginia Cross
Ann Dudley
Andrew Jackson
Barbara Kelly
Elizabeth Kinney
Reverend Esqulaira LeSure
Derlein Means
Deborah Mulberry
William Phelps
Willie Mae Reese
Claude Shields
Alfonso Smith
Charles Smith
Bill Spivery
Odessa Still

Alex Thomas
Brenda M. Ware-Abrams
Denver Wilborn
Hortense Crawford Wilborn
Regennia N. Williams, Ph.D.

Cleveland Gospel Quartet Groups

Adam Singers
AHKI Brothers
Alpha & Omega Singers
Angelic Singers
Angels of Harmony
Beams of Heaven
Bells of Joy
Blair Singers
Blue Eagles
Blue Ribbon Six
Bobby Hopkins Singers
Bright Clouds
Brownettes
Burton Gospel Singers
Burton Singers
Canaanites
Carnation Gospel Singers
Celestial Coets
Chandlier Singers

Chariot Gospel Singers
Cherubims
Chosen Consolators
Christian Brothers
Christian Travelers
Christians of Faith
Cleveland All Stars
Cleveland Coloured Quintet
Cleveland Quartet
Clevelandaires
Corinthian Singers
Crystallites
Deep River Songbirds
Delta Friendly Four
Edgerson Singers
Edmonson Sisters
Eley Sisters
Elite Jewels
Essence
Evangelistic Team
Faithful Five
Family Love Gospel Singers
Famous Glee
Five Crowns of Glory
Five Silver Kings
Flame Gospel Singers
Friendly Brothers
Friendly Five
Friendly Seven
Glover Specials
Golden Crowns
Golden Echoes
Golden Harmonettes
Golden Harmonizers
Golden Harp Gospel Singers
Golden Tones
Gospel Chosen Few
Gospel Connection
Gospel Cousins
Gospel Express
Gospel Hebrews
Gospel Hi-Risers
Gospel Imperials
Gospel Messengers
Gospel Pearls
Gospel Soloettes
Gospel Travelers
Harmonizing Queens
Harmony Echoes
Harpettes
Harps of Zion
Haymon Singers
Heavenly Wonders

Hicks Singers
Hill Singers
Howard Singers
Hubbard Singers
Humble Singers
Imperial Crowns
Imperial Jubilees
Jefferson Singers
Jesus Christ Messengers
Joynettes
Jubilee Four
Jubilee Special
King Family
King Singers
L&N Gospel Singers
Latter Rain Singers
Lauralights
Lee Adams and the Fantastics
Lee Spirituals
Levert Singers
Leviticus Singers
Lewis Singers
Little Angelettes
Little Soldiers for Christ
Little Souls for Christ
Live Wire Singers
Lockett Singers
Long Singers
Lorettaettes
Lovely Four
Mack Singers
Master Keys
McClarty Gospel Pearls
Midnight Harmonizers
Mighty Redeemers
Mighty Righteous Souls
Mighty Wings
Missionary Singers
Modernairs
Morning Stars
Munndora Singers
New Bright Clouds
New Creation
New Harpettes
New Heavenly Wonders
New Morning Stars
New Temple Spirits
North Winds
Northern Tornadoes
Northern Travelers
Ohio Silvertones
Ohio Spiritualaires
Ohio Spirituals

Ohio Traveltones
Operators
Pace Spirituals
Peace Gospel Singers
Peacock Singers
Primrose Singers
Prince of Peace Ensemble
Professor Riley and Harmony Three Plus
Queens of Harmony
Radcliffe Harmonettes
Red Rose Singers
Revelation Singers
Revelations
Revelators
Robinson Singers
Robinson Sisters
Rolling Stone
Roses of Sharon
Royal Angeletts
Royal Jubilee Singers
Ruffin Singers
Saints of Glory
Salvation Keys
Sensational Saints
Seven Revelators
Seven Souls
Shields Brothers
Silver Chimes
Silver Kings
Silvertones
Singing Crusaders
Singing Disciples
Six Gospel Writers
Smith Singers
Sons of Harmony
Sons of Joy
Sons of Truth
Soul Revivals
Soul Revivers
Soul Touchers
Sounds of Jehovah
Sounds of Soul
Southern Wonders
Spirits of Heaven
Spiritual Believers
Spiritual Blenders
Spiritual Five
Spiritual Four
Spiritual Kings
Spiritual Kings
Spiritualaires
Starlighters
Starlights

Stars of Harmony
Stars of Joy
Sunset Four
Supreme Angels
Swanee Nightingales
Sweet Chariots
Testimonial Five
Thomas Brothers
Thompkin Singers
Thompson Singers
Trinity Singers
Trojans of Joy
Trumpets of Joy
Turner Singers
Union Star Spirituals
Union Stars
Unity Singers
Vance Singers
Victory Four Quartet
Voices of Love Quartet
Voices of Love Sextet
Voices of Victory
Wade Singers
Watchingaires
Weary Four
Weary Travelers
White Singers
Williams Singers
Wilson Singers
Wise Singers
Womack Brothers
Wonders of Faith
Wondertones
Wooten Singers
World Series
Yarborough Singers
Zion Harmonizers
Zion Stars

*Gospel Music Radio Announcers,
Promoters, and Emcees*

Tommy and Earline Brooks
Dub Burton
Larry Dominic
Leroy Dye
Dynamic Promotions
Dale Edwards
Fair Promoters Club, The
Glen Curtis Frazier
LeRoy Gaynor
I.H. Gordon
Mary Holt

Curtis Shaw
Singers Journal, The
Janet Lynn Skinner
Odessa Still
William "Skippy" Still
Arthur Turner
Brenda M. Ware-Abrams
Denver Wilborn
Jerome Williams ("The Gospel Kid")
WABQ Radio
WERE Radio
WJMO Radio
WZAK Radio

BIBLIOGRAPHY

Butcher, Vada E. 1970. *A Short History of African American Gospel Music.* Washington, D.C.: Howard University.

McGhee, J. Vernon. 1982. *Thru the Bible.* Nashville, Tennessee: Thomas Nelson Publishers.

Melvin, James. 1994. *Conversations with God.* Washington, D.C.: Harper Collins Publishing.

Smith, Chas. 2001. *From Woodstock to the Moon.* Dubuque, Iowa: Kendall/Hunt Publishing Company.

The Coloured Quintette, a Narrative of God's Marvellous Dealings with the Cleveland Gospel Quintette and their Personal Testimony. 1937. John Ritchie, Ltd.

Van Tassel, David D. and John J. Grabowski, eds. 1996. *The Encyclopedia of Cleveland History.* Bloomington: Indiana University Press.

Washington, James Melvin. 1994. *Conversations with God.* New York, NY: Harper Collins Publishers.

Whelan, Ned. 1989. *Cleveland: Shaping The Vision.* Chatsworth, California: Windsor Publications, Inc.

___Williams, Regennia N. 2002. *Black America Series: Cleveland Ohio.* Chicago: Arcadia Publishing.